Water

by Margie Burton, Cathy French, and Tammy Jones

Water is all around.
You can find water
at the beach.

We use water to play.

3

You can find water
at a water fountain.

We use water to drink.

5

You can find water
in a washing machine.

We use water to wash
our clothes.

You can find water
in the bathroom.

We use water to wash
our hands.

The fire fighters use water to put out fires.

You can find water
in the kitchen.

We use water to cook.

You can find water
at the car wash.

We use water to wash the car.

How do we use water here?